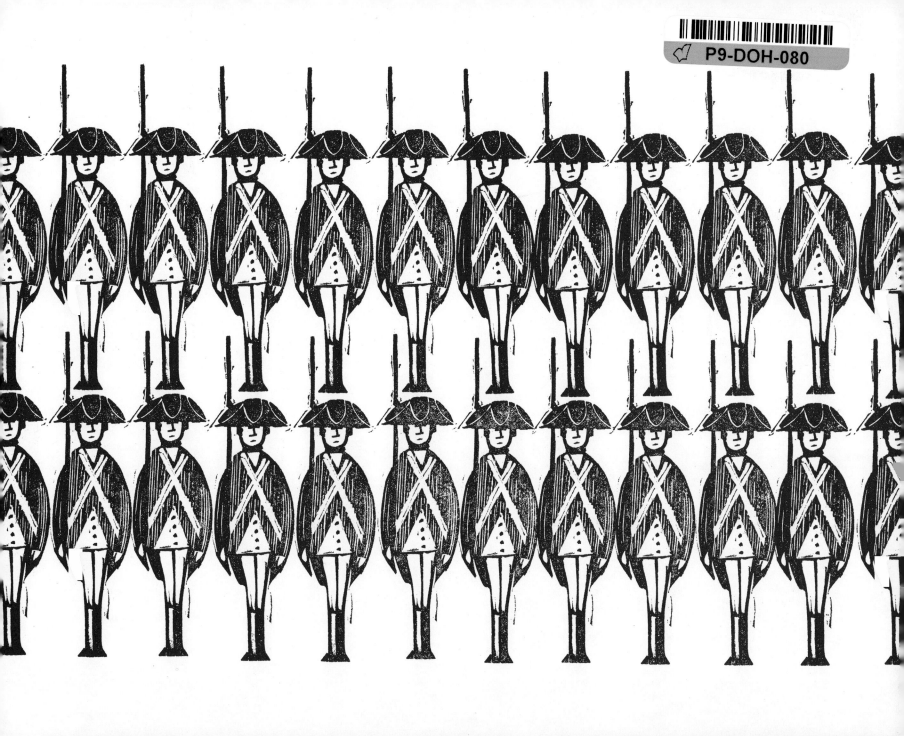

YANKEE
DOODLE

Notes by Barbara Emberley

SIMON & SCHUSTER BOOKS FOR YOUNG READERS
Published by Simon & Schuster
New York   London   Toronto   Sydney   Tokyo   Singapore

DONT TREAD ON ME

YANKEE DOODLE

By Dr. Richard Shackburg   *Woodcuts by Ed Emberley*

You may be surprised to know that YANKEE DOODLE was not written by an American. Its author was a surgeon in the British army.

The British troops sang it during the American Revolution to make fun of the rebel American troops who had no proper uniforms and of course, did not parade as prettily as the well trained British troops.

The British sang it as they marched to the Battle of Lexington where they intended to teach the rebels a lesson. However they were outsmarted at Lexington & it was the Americans who were singing Yankee Doodle as they drove the British back to Boston. It has been an American song ever since.

Here are a few more things you might like to know about this song: The word YANKEE is thought to come from the Indians. When they tried to pronounce English, it came out "Yengees" which soon became Yankees. The word DOODLE used to mean "a silly person" & still means "flute" in German.

In those days the word MACARONI meant very fancy trimming, like gold braid, ribbons, & plumes. It came from a group of English dandies called "Macaroni" who used to wear a lot of gold braid, ribbons & plumes and met regularly to eat an exotic dish called macaroni.

General George Washington is called CAPTAIN Washington in the song simply because he had not been promoted to General when the song was first written.

HASTY PUDDING is a very thick pudding. Try it and see.

Put in a double boiler top 2 cups boiling water & stir in,

1/3 cup corn meal

1/2 teaspoon salt

Cook over hot water till thick (about one hour) stirring occasionally. Serve with butter & finely shaved maple sugar.

And now, meet Yankee Doodle.....

Yankee Doodle went to town, riding on a pony

Stuck a feather in his hat and called it macaroni.

Yankee Doodle keep it up, Yankee Doodle dandy;

Mind the music and the step, and with the girls be handy.

Father and I went down to camp, along with Captain Good'in.

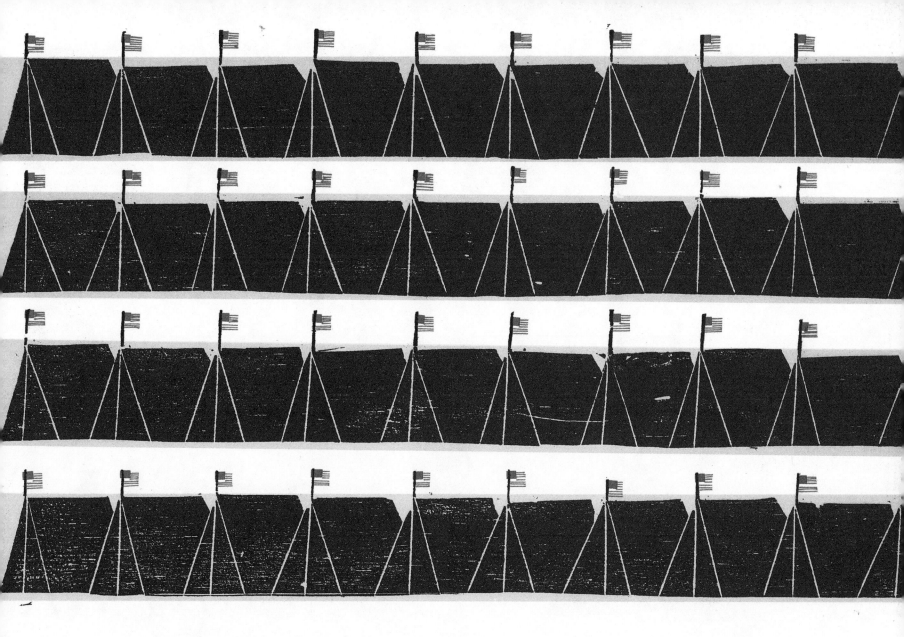

❁❁

And there we saw the men and boys as thick as hasty puddin'.

And there we saw a thousand men, as rich as Squire David;

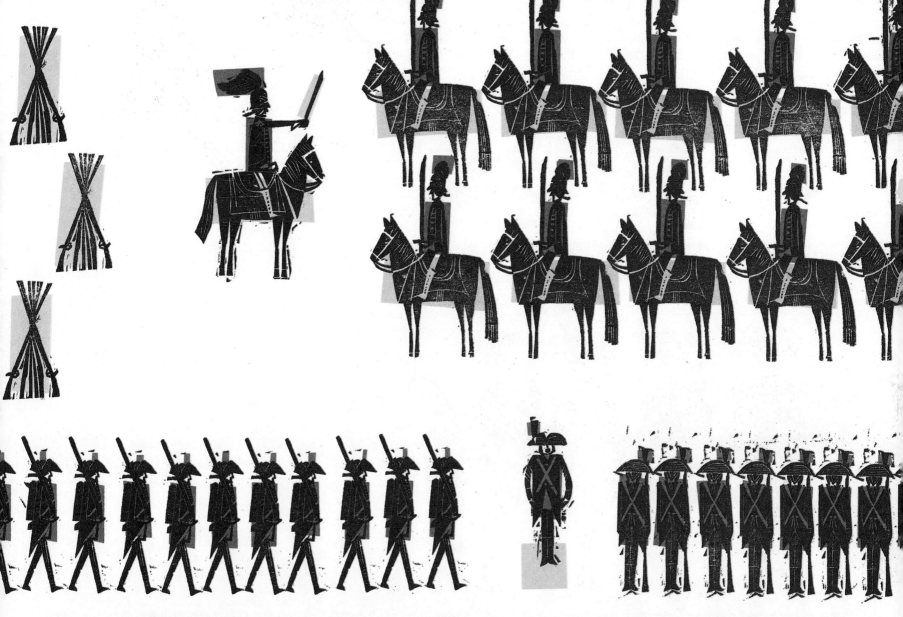

And what they wasted ev'ry day, I wish it could be saved.

And there I saw a little keg, its head all made of leather,

They knocked on it with little sticks, to call the folks together.

And there was Captain Washington upon a slapping stallion,

A giving orders to his men; I guess there was a million.

And the ribbons on his hat, they looked so very fine, ah!

I wanted peskily to get to give to my Jemima.

And there I saw a swamping gun, large as a log of maple

Upon a mighty little cart; a load for father's cattle.

And every time they fired it off, it took a horn of powder;

It made a noise like father's gun, only a nation louder.

The troopers, too, would gallop up and fire right in our faces;

It scared me almost half to death to see them run such races.

It scared me so I hooked it off, nor stopped, as I remember,

Nor turned about till I got home, locked up in mother's chamber.

Yankee Doodle

Yankee Doodle went to town,
Riding on a pony;
Stuck a feather in his hat
And called it Macaroni.

Chorus
Yankee Doodle keep it up,
Yankee Doodle dandy;
Mind the Music and the step,
And with the girls be handy.

Father and I went down to camp,
Along with Captain Good'in,
And there we saw the men and boys
As thick as has-ty pud-din'.
(Chorus)

And there we saw a thousand men,
As rich as Squire David;
And what they wasted ev'ry day,
I wish it could be sav'ed.
(Chorus)

And there I saw a little keg,
Its head all made of leather,
They knocked on it with little sticks,
To call the folks together.
(Chorus)

And there was Captain Washington
Upon a slapping stallion,
A-giving orders to his men;
I guess there was a million.
(Chorus)

And the ribbons on his hat,
They looked so very fine, ah!
I wanted peskily to get
To give to my Jemima.
(Chorus)

And there I saw a swamping gun,
Large as a log of maple,
Upon a mighty little cart;
A load for father's cattle
(Chorus)

And every time they fired it off,
It took a horn of powder;
It made a noise like father's gun,
Only a nation louder.
(Chorus)

The troopers, too, would gallop up
And fire right in our faces;
It scared me almost half to death
To see them run such races.
(Chorus)

It scared me so I hooked it off,
Nor stopped, as I remember,
Nor turned about till I got home,
Locked up in mother's chamber.
(Chorus)

Original words sung by the English are generally
attributed to Dr. Richard Schackburg but the authors
of the American version have never been determined

American Folk
Arrangement, CHARITY BAILEY

Music from a popular
18th century air

Yan-kee Doo-dle went to town, A-rid-ing on a po-ny; Stuck a feath-er in his hat and called it mac-a-ro-ni.

Chorus

Yan-kee Doo-dle, keep it up, Yan-kee Doo-dle Dan-dy, Mind the Mus-ic and the step, And with the girls be hand-y.

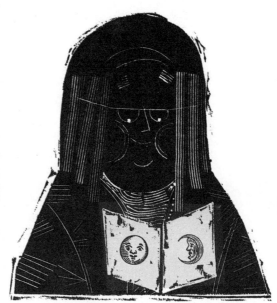

The TYPE

❊❊❊❊❊❊❊❊❊❊❊❊❊❊❊❊❊

The type for this book was hand set &
printed on a small hand press (a 6" x 9"
Golding) by the artist.
This is the same type (Caslon Old Face)
cast by the same foundry (The Caslon
Letter Foundry, Sheffield, England)
which supplied Ben Franklin with type
"Sufficient for an ALMANACK."
"Caslon" was quite popular with the
American colonial printers . It was used
to print Bibles, broadsides, the current
ballads like *YANKEE DOODLE*
& all sorts of things including the
Declaration of Independence.

SIMON & SCHUSTER BOOKS FOR YOUNG READERS, 1230 Avenue of the Americas, New York, New York 10020. Copyright © 1965 by Edward Emberley. Originally published in 1965 by Prentice Hall. First Simon & Schuster hardcover edition, 1994. All rights reserved including the right of reproduction in whole or in part in any form. SIMON & SCHUSTER BOOKS FOR YOUNG READERS is a trademark of Simon & Schuster. Also available in a HALF MOON BOOKS paperback edition. The text for this book is set in Caslon 540. The illustrations were done in woodcut. Manufactured in the United States of America 10 9 8 7 6 5 4 3 2 1
Library of Congress Cataloging-in-Publication Data: Schackburg, Richard. Yankee Doodle / by Richard Schackburg ; woodcuts by Ed Emberley. p.   cm.   Summary : This version of the song popularized during the Revolution features woodcuts of the American and British armies.   1. Children's songs—United States—Texts. 2. United States—History—Revolution, 1775-1783—Songs and music. [1. Songs—United States. 2. United States—History—Revolution, 1775-1783—Songs and music.] I. Emberley, Ed, ill. II. Title PZ8.3.S285Yan 1993 782.42164'0268—dc20 93-28633 CIP AC ISBN: 0-671-88559-6 (HC)   ISBN: 0-671-88645-2 (PBK)

ABOUT THE FLAGS IN THIS BOOK

The artist has used several regimental flags, such as the Bunker Hill flag and a version of the serpent flag, which were carried by our troops during The Revolutionary War. He has, however, chosen to highlight the thirteen-starred flag because it is the historical symbol of the American fight for freedom. It is this flag which became our national flag in 1777.

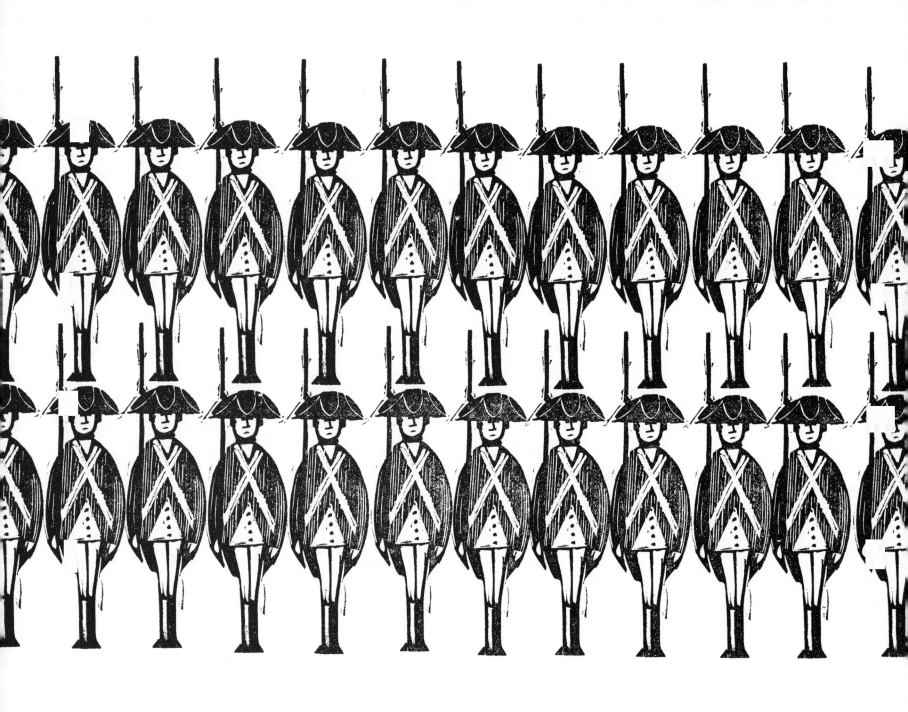